Resolution

Solution

2017

3 Easy Steps to Achieve Your Goals

CHRIS WEILER

MythBuster Media Inc
Chicago

Copyright © 2017 by Chris Weiler

Books may be purchased in quantity and/or special sales by contacting the publisher.

Mythbuster Media Inc.
Chicago
sales@MythBusterMedia.com
www.MythBusterMedia.com

Library of Congress Control Number: 2017900171

ISBN 0-9891796-4-8
ISBN 978-0-9891796-4-5
Cover Design: Gion-Per Marxer - Gion-Per@BeeCoding.com

Contents

Introduction

My objective is to provide you with the most efficient and effective method to succeed in your goals. To this end, I will share with you my 3 step process that will provide the missing link to your success.

In most cases, the unmet items on your resolution list exist because you have conditioned reflexive behaviors that oppose your efforts. By following the three actionable steps in this book, you will create new reflexive habits to support succeeding in your resolutions.

Pay close attention to Chapter 4, where you will discover why most people (92%) fail in their resolutions.

I wrote this book as a lean and efficient guide for the *just tell me what to do, make it easy* and *make it work* crowd. If you want a very detailed, in-depth breakdown on how to achieve goals, get my book *The Reflex* - *Activate Thoughts, Words and Actions to Achieve Your Goals.*

Quick note about myself. I am a performance expert to athletes, Fortune 500's and YOU.

Let's Do It!

Chapter 1

Step One - Do This First

The first and most crucial step is to create a **Guiding Principle**. Simply state a concept, ideal or way of being that directly or indirectly anchors you to your resolution. **Guiding Principles** are best expressed as values driven statements such as Family First, Education First, Health First, Career First, Patience, Compassion, How Can I Help You, or Pay it Forward. Any religious or philosophical tenets are also good examples. A **Guiding Principle (GP)** represents a priority in your life, enabling the empowerment of both yourself and others.

Guiding Principles are what you believe and put your faith in. They provide a lens to focus and express your thoughts, words and actions through. **Guiding Principles** shape how you perceive yourself, other people, circumstances and the world around you.

Guiding Principles keep your *attention* on the *intention* of your goal, by keeping you focused on what is required to support your resolution.

Think of your **Guiding Principle** as a bridge enabling you to transport your resolution from concept to completion.

Without this bridge, you must rely on willpower or short term inspiration and motivation. These rarely have the capacity to achieve lasting change or weather the storm when faced with obstacles between you and your goal.

Personally, I visualize driving a stake or flag into the ground to represent my **Guiding Principles**. This imagery plants a fixed point of reference in my mind and heart, with the power to create and attract thoughts, words and actions to support those principles.

Having your first child is an example of a fixed point in one's life. Most people take this opportunity to define **Guiding Principles** of how they will act as parents to guide their child's development.

The nature of a child, to be dependent on others to survive, when aligned with the parent's **Guiding Principles**, automatically attracts a lifestyle in the form of thoughts, words and actions to support their **Guiding Principles**, while at the same time eliminating things that oppose these values.

It then follows, we begin to struggle when we do not have practices in place to help create thoughts, words and actions that align with our principles.

Create Your Guiding Principle

Now that you understand the value and power of **Guiding Principles** - choose one. What is your fixed point of reference that will help attract thoughts, words and actions to stay the course in achieving your goals? Don't worry about choosing a perfect one, as you can always modify it later. For now simply go with your reflex, your gut. What is your first thought or feeling that is triggered when asked to choose a **Guiding Principle**? Write down your **Guiding Principle** - Now.

Serves Many Masters

Guiding Principles are not mutually exclusive from one another. One principle can serve different objectives depending on whether they are directly or indirectly applied.

For example, a direct application of the Family First principle can mean your direct objective is to prioritize the needs of your family, such as being a better listener, financial provider, or spending more time together. Used indirectly however, a Family First principle can help prioritize your weight loss, health or fitness goals.

In your heart and mind, associate how your personal goal benefits your family, by placing your *attention* on the *intention* of your **Guiding Principle** and goal. How? Simply focus on creating thoughts, words and actions that support the values of your **Guiding Principle.** Said another way, add thoughts words and actions that support your Guiding Principle and goal, and subtract those that oppose.

This means financial, fitness or weight loss goals can support a resolution to show more patience and compassion to one's family. Losing weight and getting fit directly help you look, feel and move better in your daily life. Reduced stress, increased energy and better sleep are additional ways you benefit. When you feel good within yourself, you feel happy. Your happiness enables you to create thoughts, words and actions that indirectly support your Family First values. The direct benefits you receive by achieving your weight loss and getting fit resolution, also increase your capacity to give to your family.

It's all connected!

When I say, *in your heart and mind...*, I mean what is honest, true and authentic for you. A client of mine says she exercises to have *a kick-ass body so she can make her friends and co-workers jealous.* Her goal and the principle that guides it is authentic for her. She is proud of it and will yell it from the rooftops. Some of you reading this might also *THINK* you would like a body that others are envious of, but if you do not really *FEEL* that way, you will never create the necessary thoughts, words and actions required to drive that goal to success.

This explains why two people can be observed performing the exact same actions towards a goal, yet only one succeeds. Those who succeed have their actions strongly anchored to a feeling that is the by-product of a principle that has personal value, which I call a **Guiding Principle**. The one who fails is merely prompted to take action by an idea. An idea that lacks a strong emotional base or deep personal value. Sure, I'd like the benefits of that goal (provided it doesn't take too much effort or time). Your family, friends, co-workers, the media and conventional wisdom all might value a specific goal citing, *this is what an educated person of my age, who lives in my zip code SHOULD value.* But if you personally do not feel this way, then you cannot value that goal and you will continue to struggle.

Each thought, word and action either supports or opposes our **Guiding Principles** and therefore, goals. When faced with an opportunity to choose between that which supports or opposes your efforts, put your *attention* on the object of your *intention*, your **Guiding Principle** and resolution.

For example, a Family First **Guiding Principle** means you place your *attention* on your *intention* to support your Family First **Guiding Principle**. This crucial step is the missing link to resolution success. Each time your thoughts, words and actions support your **Guiding Principle**, you make deposits to your behavioral bank account, making it easier to withdraw the funds that support those habits the next time, moving you one step closer to resolution victory.

Don't worry, in the coming pages I will show you how to connect the dots between the goal you commit to in your heart and mind, and the physical action steps necessary to power your **Guiding Principle** and succeed in your goal.

Intention

Guiding Principles are driven by purposeful intention. Without the focused intention of a purpose, you are detached from what you feel and believe in your heart - your Authentic Self. If you only care about the benefits of a goal and not the process required to achieve it, then you lack the required intention to support, drive and motivate you to endure the process.

Said another way, when your heart does not *feel like* there is any purpose to the process, your resolution efforts become *half-hearted*. When you struggle with your thoughts, words and actions in support of your resolution, it is because you have not established a **Guiding Principle** to plug your purposeful intent into. Therefore, failure is likely as you are subject to whatever reflexive responses are tied to your existing habits and behaviors.

Emotion Creates *Motion*

Motivation cannot be acquired externally, but must be developed from within when we are emotionally *moved* or inspired. Without a value driven **Guiding Principle**, your resolutions become solely benefits driven (what you will get at the end), which is why you lack the motivation to see your resolutions through.

Of course we all want the benefits, but keeping your attention and your heart on the principles and values those benefits are tied to, is what distinguishes those who fail from those who succeed.

A wonderful Buddhist monk I studied with named Gen Khedrub said to me, *change and fulfillment only occur when we move what we think from the level of our head down to our heart and mix it with our emotions.* The idea may start in the mind, but until it is mixed with your heart, your emotions, how you feel, it lacks the required power to create meaningful, lasting change or fulfillment. Said another way, Emotion Creates *Motion.*

What About Carrot Chasers?

At the time of this writing, I am running an exercise challenge at The Tennis and Fitness Centre in Oak Park, Illinois called Resolution Solution 2017. Since I planned this book and challenge at the same time... same name.

As we started the challenge before an official prize list was posted, a few members informed me they had not yet joined since there was not a prize list to see what they were working towards. Classic carrot chasing tied to external motivation. What do I get?

And, as long as this aligns with your authentic self - great! How do you know if it aligns or not? Ask yourself if you are often motivated by external rewards. Are you usually successful? If so, your carrot chasing habit is likely anchored to a value you feel strongly about and you probably view the world through a work/reward lens. But if achieving goals was as easy as hanging a reward in front of us, then why do so many people still not succeed? The power for motivation and taking action is not in the carrot/reward, but whether or not that carrot/reward triggers a powerful emotional response within YOU. This explains why 2 people can be working for the same reward, but only one does what is necessary and follows it through to the end.

Use Your Religion

For those of you who are religious, incorporate your religion in your **Guiding Principle**. Get organized, lose weight, address your finances, find love or put your relationships first by creating thoughts, words and actions that better enable you to help others in the name of your religious tenets. Specifically, put your *attention* on taking daily actionable steps that move you closer to your resolution, with the *intention* that success in your goal will allow you to better express your religious values.

When the religious beliefs in your heart, couple with the resolutions in your head, they immaculately conceive an offspring that empowers you to achieve your goals and better support your religious principles. (C'mon, some of you are giggling at that one)!

It's all connected.

To be clear, I do not generally support or oppose using religion in crafting your **Guiding Principle**. Specifically, I support is what is important to you, what YOU value, in your heart. If it is religion, wonderful - use it. If not, also wonderful - use something else.

Resolution Reality Check

Goals are NOT achieved directly. They are indirect by-products of your daily habits and rituals - your lifestyle. **Guiding Principles** keep you connected to a values driven lifestyle capable of achieving your goals.

For those of you still procrastinating on creating a **Guiding Principle**, do it now. You will need it for the final two steps, which we will cover next.

Chapter 2

Steps Two and Three - Do These Daily

We are what we repeatedly do.
Excellence, then, is not an act, but a habit. - Aristotle

In this chapter we will uncover the two daily action steps that will create a bridge between your **Guiding Principle** and resolution. Much like the experience with bumper bowling, where guide rails keep your ball out of the gutter assuring you hit at least one pin, these two actions serve as behavior guide rails, assuring you keep on track to fulfill your resolutions.

1. Check Your Mind

Discover what you think and feel when you are conflicted between doing something that opposes rather than supports your goal.

How it Works

This is performed silently, so it can be done anywhere, anytime. Simply **Check Your Mind** to discover what you think and feel at any given moment, but especially when you feel stressed or conflicted between thoughts, words and actions that do not support your resolution. Be honest, as there is no right or wrong answer. Personally, I check my mind throughout the day while driving, writing, during conversation and shopping.

Perhaps you are trying to diet and know you should be following a proper nutrition model, like the one found in my nutrition book **The 3/4 Rule**. However, you are craving foods that don't support or will sabotage your diet goals. This is the time to **Check Your Mind** and discover the thoughts and feelings that drive and nourish those cravings. Whatever thoughts and feelings you discover - name them.

The next step is to decide if you like what you think or feel. Do they align with your values, your **Guiding Principle**? Again, no wrong or right answer, simply what is right or wrong for YOU.

Perhaps you have been eating a balanced diet and meeting your exercise goals for the past 3 weeks. So, you **Check Your Mind** and discover that you *feel* pretty good about your craving for that 600 calorie dessert. However, if you *don't feel good about it*, yet still submit to your craving, you are reinforcing habits that may sabotage your efforts and set you up for failure. You cannot simply rely on intellectual justification, as the power lies in how you *feel*, and you need to *feel good* about it. This is how we align the Mind, Body and Heart, and condition them to create thoughts, words and actions that best support our future efforts.

Whenever you **Check Your Mind** and discover you do not like what you think or feel, name a thought or feeling that opposes it, and supports the thoughts, feelings and reflexive habits you want to reinforce. This simply requires you conduct yourself in a way that reflects the thoughts, words and actions you want to develop.

For example, let's imagine I have just finished eating all the food on my plate while at a family holiday meal, and out of habit or because it's the holiday, I ready myself to get a second, third or fourth serving.

However, I stop to **Check My Mind** and discover although I feel like eating more, as I am conditioned to associate food with increasing my happiness and satisfaction while socializing, I am conflicted and therefore do not feel good about my actions opposing my **Guiding Principle** and resolution. I attempt to justify my actions with internal dialogue such as, *It's the holidays, I'm with family and friends, I want to feel free to enjoy myself and not feel restricted for just one day*. I can justify my actions with every logically persuasive argument available, and yet none of it is relevant if I do not feel good about my actions. When I take action, yet do not feel good about it, I fracture the foundation that supports my efforts at achieving my goals. Repeated fractures will destroy my goals.

In this instance I can create thoughts and feelings that support my resolution by placing my *attention* on my *intention* to acquire these same unrestricted feelings of enjoyment I normally associate with food, by engaging with others and focusing on their needs. Did you catch the subtle, yet powerful shift that just occurred? It happened when I shifted my attention away from myopically satisfying my own needs, which for some reason require food to fulfill, and focusing on the needs of others.

To not risk bogging you down with biochemistry, let's just say, the type and quantity of bio-chemicals produced are different when focused inwardly on myself, than when externally focused on others. The power of this bio-chemical shift disengages the flow of chemicals nourishing my habits that oppose my goals.

There is no universal right or wrong answer, just what is right or wrong for you. This means you could be sitting at the table with me in my holiday meal example, and share my exact same resolution, yet it is okay for me to get multiple servings, while it is not the correct action for you. What each of us privately thinks and feels need to be in alignment or we will fail in our resolutions.

From productivity at work, to communication issues with family, friends, co-workers, bosses or employees, to challenges with anger, stress or depression, to problems with personal finance, **Checking Your Mind** will unveil the subconscious triggers that disrupt your ability to put your *attention* on the *intention* of your **Guiding Principle**. **Checking Your Mind** enables you to successfully navigate the path to your resolution's destination.

Why it Works

We need to synchronize our habits and actions with what is written in our subconscious minds. If there is not a script that reflexively cues you to take action in support of your goals, failure becomes more likely.

Checking Your Mind breaks your reflexive response pattern. This action increases the gap between moments, and the interval between one reflexive response that opposes your success and another. Questioning how you think and feel, requires you to be present and in the moment, enabling you to uncover and address the root of your self-sabotaging behavior.

Not limited to deterrence, the power of **Checking Your Mind** also reinforces thoughts, words and actions that align with your **Guiding Principle**, making it easier to access them again. What I have just described is the birth, care and feeding of a habit.

Understand that **Checking Your Mind** is both about how you think and feel. You might only be aware of what you think in a given moment, but recognize there is always an emotion tied to your thought - always! Some of you will need to dig deeper than others to root it out.

2. Compose Yourself

The final step of our Resolution Success model is a simple writing exercise designed to remove subconscious barriers that oppose your resolutions, while creating the causes for thoughts, words and actions that support your resolutions.

How it Works

With 2-3 blank sheets of paper, begin writing as fast as you can whatever is in your head. DO NOT judge, worry about grammar, punctuation, legibility or try to make it about anything specific. This is a free flow, subconscious mind dump, from your head to paper. Curse, be profane, prolific, happy, angry, sad or silly. Let whatever is in you flow uninterrupted from pen to paper. Feel free to begin by writing how weird you think this exercise is. What you write does not need to make sense, and might look or feel like inane ramblings - it's all good! When finished, shred or file your writing and move on with your day.

Although you can **Compose Yourself** anytime, it has a more profound impact immediately after waking in the morning, before you interface with any person or technology. This means before email, phone or TV.

You heard me, BEFORE email or phone. Close your eyes and take a breath - you can do it!

Why it Works

This is a daily, subconscious house cleaning, that first brings awareness, then helps loosen and remove the harmful deposits in your subconscious mind. These damaging deposits create and reinforce habits that contribute to poor performance. You see, the conscious mind references the subconscious mind for most of our conscious actions.

Our past and current thoughts, words and actions are deposited into the subconscious mind. These deposits are reflexively used to shape our future thoughts, words and actions. Much like a checking account, whatever deposits have been made, are what is available for withdrawal.

A Bit More on Composing Yourself

Ideally, plan on **Composing Yourself** for 3 pages. It often requires this amount of space and time to go deep enough to loosen the entrenched thoughts and deeply embedded baggage deposited in your subconscious mind.

At times however, you may be genuinely done after 2 pages, and have nothing else to write. There are also times when you are short on time and simply need to stop. That's okay, as the process of changing behaviors and habits is cumulative. Feel proud and satisfied you took the few moments you had to **Compose Yourself**, rather than justify blowing it off because something else came up, and you plan to *do it later*. Of course there are times when this will happen, so **Check Your Mind** to honestly distinguish between your legitimate and illegitimate reasons.

Action Steps

Another powerful way to **Compose Yourself**, which goes beyond a subconscious house cleaning, is to integrate action steps. Action steps are bridges that connect your thoughts and words to your goal. Driven by and an extension of the thoughts and words you choose, your action steps either support or oppose your efforts. **Check Your Mind.**

Sure, you have plans to save money, quit smoking, stop procrastinating, get married, get divorced, start your business or lose weight. So, what actionable steps have you taken to bridge the gap between your schemes, dreams, and desired outcome?

First

Check Your Mind to discover what you think or feel when you are stressed, angry, depressed, not productive, procrastinating, or experiencing any thoughts, words or actions that oppose your **Guiding Principle** and/or goal. There is no right or wrong answer, simply an honest unveiling of the subconscious triggers that create obstacles between you and your happiness.

Second

Name the thoughts and/or feelings discovered in the first step above and write them down on a piece of paper. Be Concise, choosing as few words as possible.

Third

Choose one or more words that counter or oppose the thoughts and feelings you wrote above and write them down. Break out the thesaurus if you need help. WordHippo.com is a great website for this.

Fourth

Building Bridges. Write down ONE action step that physically connects you to your goal and moves you one step closer to integrating it into your life. Ex. Sign up for class. Get up and run a 1/4 mile. Make that call. Have that conversation. Read that book. Make that budget. Now write this action step over and over until you fill up the page. When finished, get up and do it - NOW!

Repeat the process tomorrow with another action step. Adding a pebble a day to a jar at first seems insignificant, but the cumulative effect is quickly recognized.

Why This Works

This version of **Compose Yourself** adds the additional element of **Action Steps**. Since many of us get bogged down at this critical juncture between thought and action, this exercise enables us to successfully bridge that gap. The cumulative effect of taking small, seemingly insignificant daily actions is the secret to great accomplishments.

Chapter 3

Let's Review

Create a principles-driven, **Guiding Principle** that will help attract thoughts, words and actions enabling you to stay the course and achieve your resolutions.

Check Your Mind to discover what you think and feel about any thoughts, words or actions that relate to your resolution. Decide if they support or oppose your resolution. Do you feel good or bad? If you don't feel good, name the thought and feeling you would like to replace it with and perform some action that supports and expresses that thought and feeling.

Compose Yourself. With 2-3 blank sheets of paper, begin writing as fast as you can whatever is in your head. DO NOT judge, worry about grammar, punctuation, legibility or try to make it about anything specific. This is a free flow, subconscious mind dump, from your head to paper. Shred your writing or file it for future reference, the choice is yours.

Compose Yourself with Action Steps.

a. Name and write down the feelings and thoughts discovered when you **Checked Your Mind**. Be concise, choosing as few words as possible.

b. If what you write does not support your Guiding Principle, choose one or more words that oppose those thoughts and feelings and write them down.

c. Write down ONE action step that physically connects you to your resolution and moves you one step closer to integrating it into your lifestyle. As fast as possible, write this action step over and over until you fill the page. Get up and perform that action step - NOW!

d. Repeat this process as needed to stay the course.

Weight loss, health, fitness, finances, education, relationship and mental/emotional goals are all governed by one common element - conditioned reflexes. You see, the conscious mind references the subconscious mind to produce the majority of one's thoughts, words and actions. Good or bad, whatever you have deposited into your subconscious mind, is what is reflexively available for the conscious mind to withdraw.

Understanding that the circular relationship between the conscious and subconscious mind is similar to a checking account, dependent on a system of deposits and withdrawals, helps demystify the interplay between these parts of the brain.

As with a physical checking account, the funds available for withdrawal are dependent on the funds that have been deposited. People who succeed in their resolutions, make deposits to their subconscious mind, capable of producing behaviors that support their objectives. Those who fail, simply make deposits that oppose their efforts.

Every thought you generate, word you speak and action you take, either supports or opposes your resolution success - period. **Checking Your Mind** and **Composing Yourself** keep you anchored to your **Guiding Principle**s and achieving what is important to you in life.

Chapter 4

Why We Fail

We are what we repeatedly do.
Excellence, then, is not an act, but a habit. - Aristotle

Aristotle's quote is as relevant here as it is in Chapter Two, which is why it is repeated. Resolutions are NOT achieved directly. They are indirect by-products of your daily habits and rituals - your lifestyle. The problem is that we are creatures of immediate gratification with magic-bullet mentalities. We are seduced by quick fixes, sound-bite advice and solutions provided in 140 characters or less. While these abbreviated actions may give us the illusory perception we are keeping pace with the social currency of the day, it also makes those solutions cheap, disposable and therefore, not valuable or helpful in meeting our goals.

To help you avoid the common obstacles that interfere with achieving your goals, this chapter will uncover the four most toxic, yet subtle elements that destroy our resolution resolve.

Reason #1 - Consumerism

I am comfortable saying, *consumerism is the root of all resolution evil*, as the other reasons given in this chapter that create obstacles on your path to resolution success, all stem from consumerism.

The Short Explanation:

- We suffer from consumerism.

- When not consuming, we spend many of our waking hours planning what to consume and acquiring that which enables us to consume, including work, money, food and attention.

- As such, many of us look at ourselves, other people and life in general, through the filtered eyes of a consumer.

- We the consumer have been conditioned to search outside of the mind, body and heart, within the consumer market, for solutions to both personal goals and societal problems. This approach often fails, as consumer goods and services are rarely capable of inspiring us to *feel like* taking the necessary steps to achieve our goals.

- When your heart and mind are in alignment, they create motivation, desire and passion, empowering you to stay the course until you reach your goals. This is the secret to fulfilling your resolutions. The consumer market cannot give you this, as motivation, desire and passion cannot be consumed or acquired through external sources.

The Longer Explanation:

The majority of people are conditioned from birth to be consumers. In fact, while being resold the American Dream, our post World War II government made it clear an American's primary duty was to be a consumer. Not surprising when you consider the fiscal toll that war took on our economy.

However, our conditioned consumer habits often oppose personally meaningful goals and resolutions. The inherent problem is that resolutions, often enmeshed with personal development and happiness, cannot be acquired through *consumerism*. Contrary to their marketing claims, you cannot lose weight, get fit, find love, quit smoking or improve your finances through the consumption of goods and services, until both your head and heart are in alignment.

Your heart creates the motivation to drive the resolutions in your head to completion. The consumer market attempts to bypass this head/heart relationship by convincing you to purchase a readymade solution to achieve your resolution. *Consumerism* is simply the wrong tool for the job.

As with any tool, consumer goods and services have no power to give you anything until acted upon by YOU. Your mind, heart, intention and skill all determine whether you use your hammer to build something wonderful or destroy something beautiful. Common consumer tools to help our resolutions include to join a club, hire a trainer, start a new fad diet, sign up for online dating or slap on that nicotine patch. Oh... and buy books like the one you are reading now.

Sure, come January you can follow the rest of the weight loss resolution herd into fitness centers and health clubs across the nation. Your short lived motivation will last until about February, when the herd retreats back to their familiar, non-exercise habits. The regulars at the gym will say to each other, *glad that's over until next January.*

The point is, until you have done the internal work, such as develop a **Guiding Principle** and reinforce its use by **Checking Your Mind** and **Composing Yourself**, you may not have the capacity, drive and motivation to use your consumer tools in a way that will ensure you succeed in your resolutions.

To be clear, this is not an indictment on capitalism. However, it is important to understand how our conditioned consumer reflexes often conflict with our goals.

Many people find this distinction difficult as they have only looked at the world through the eyes of a consumer. We spend the majority of our first 25 years of life, being pushed through an educational system that was primarily constructed for one purpose - to get a job. From the economy's perspective, our jobs serve the distinct function of enabling our ability to purchase and consume goods and services, which are *supposed to make us happy*. You know, the white picket fence and so forth.

Since the marketplace exists to buy and sell, it can only define happiness in context of its architecture - acquisition and consumption - thereby reinforcing its own existence and needs. What about your personal needs, thoughts and feelings that transcend the limitations of the latest version of a product or service?

Are most of these goods and services relevant and valuable in context of your Authentic Self, what you personally require to be happy or achieve your goals?

How would you know?

The consumer marketing machine is only concerned with satisfying your Consumer Self, the result of which has conditioned a set of wants and needs that do not necessarily reflect the needs and wants of your Authentic Self.

The misalignment between one's Authentic Self and Consumer Self are where many people's resolution efforts get derailed. The consumer marketplace has created a list of items for you to choose from when making your how to have a happy life checklist, which typically includes the right job, house, spouse, kids, zip code, car, clothing, appearance, personal accessories and technology. The question begged, do my choices in these areas support my Authentic Self or my Consumer Self?

Although we are conditioned to relate to much of what we see in terms of consumption, goals and happiness are processes that require development, and development cannot be acquired solely by consumption of goods and services.

The marketplace simply does not and cannot sell what is required to achieve these things unless you honestly have a passionate connection to those goods and services that inspires motivation.

The most important areas of lives, where we spend the most time, money and effort, require years of development including relationships, education, occupation, personal and physical growth. It then follows and comes as no surprise, those who try to shortcut or bypass development, typically fail in achieving their goals.

The *thing* Has No Power - You Do!

Have you ever wondered why some people succeed in their resolutions, while others fail, yet they use the exact same consumer driven product or service? As is true with any tool, the diet, gym, fitness app, dating service, or self-help book, have little power to give you anything until powered by YOU. **The *thing* Has No Power - You Do**, is what distinguishes those who attain their resolutions from those who do not, and reinforces the point of this book. To achieve your resolution, empower it with a **Guiding Principle**, as this is what creates motivation to succeed. Unless the truth is, you honestly *don't feel like it*. We will address this next.

Reason #2 - <u>I Don't Feel Like It</u>

Emotion creates *motion*. This means we are motivated to take action on what we feel or *feel like* doing. When what we think about our resolution is in alignment with how we feel about our resolution, we succeed. It then follows, failure occurs when what we think and feel are not in alignment. The primary reason people do not succeed in their resolutions...

They simply *don't feel like it*.

Our basic rational for why we do or do not do something, has not changed much from when we were 5 years old. When we are young and don't want to do something, we simply say, *I don't wanna!* When pressed further for an answer, we have one additional layer of introspection available by explaining, because *I don't feel like it*.

Regardless of our age, the reality is that mostly we do something because we *feel like it*, or don't do something because we *don't feel like it*.

Sure, some of you are thinking, I do plenty of things I *don't feel like* doing including work, school, household and family obligations. Take a moment and reflect on your daily responsibilities and obligations, the things you feel you do for others. Part of this list will undoubtedly include things you *don't feel like* doing, but do anyway.

With this in mind, I challenge you to explain why you do these things, without using the words *I, ME, MY, OUR,* or including any physical, mental or emotional benefit to yourself. You will find this a nearly impossible task.

You might not *feel like* working, but you do so because you *feel like* receiving the benefits it provides for yourself and the people you care about. As parents, we are often in the position of doing things we *don't feel like* doing. I *don't feel like* driving my daughter to her friends house, spending six hours at a gymnastics meet, track meet, choir concert, violin recital or attending team and school fundraisers.

I do however, *feel like* supporting one of my **Guiding Principles,** to aid in the development of a compassionate, happy, healthy, thinking person, that I love with all my heart. So when she asks me to drive her to a friends house, I put my *attention* on my **Guiding Principle,** with the *intention* of contributing to my daughters happiness and healthy social development.

The result is an alignment of my thoughts, words and actions with my **Guiding Principle**, which enables me to *feel like* driving her. Said another way, I put my *attention* on my love for her, which creates feelings that motivate me to take action. This is a very different dynamic, which produces very different feelings, than simply supporting my daughter out of reflexive duty and obligation. Unless, I feel driven by a strong personal value of duty and obligation.

In case you missed it, the paragraph above explains exactly how to apply **Guiding Principles** and integrate them into your heart and mind. Please re-read.

Weight Loss

Unless you have a metabolic, physical, or hormonal disorder, or limited by certain prescription medication, you lose weight because you want to lose weight. Conversely, if you cannot lose weight and maintain it, you simply *don't feel like it* - enough. As I said, emotion creates motion, and we are motivated to take action when we *feel like it*.

That's right, I said if you cannot lose weight, and keep a personally acceptable amount off long term, then you honestly do not want to achieve your weight loss goals bad enough. More specifically, you are not emotionally invested enough to *feel* sufficiently motivated to alter or create a lifestyle that supports your goal. Sure, you want the end result, the benefits, but not bad enough to put in the required effort. You also might enjoy the benefits of owning your own business, but are you willing to do what is necessary to achieve that end?

Many people are not, which is why there will always be another fat loss *tip, trick* or *hack* available for your consumption. Simply put, most people who do not succeed in their goals *don't feel like* doing what is necessary to achieve results.

If your weight loss resolution is primarily benefits driven, meaning to receive compliments, fit into certain clothes and improve your social currency, you will likely fail.

Benefits that solely feed your ego, rarely have the power to create sustained motivation unless you feel very passionately about those benefits. The narcissists who prioritize how they look over everything else in life succeed because they live by a **Guiding Principle** of aesthetics. Remember, **Guiding Principles** do not have to be *principled*. Passion perseveres!

The more passionately you feel about something, the more likely your success - good or bad. Consider how passionate terrorists are about their ends. The point is, resolution success happens when your feelings are in alignment with your thoughts, words and actions, thus producing the required motivation to see it through to completion.

In case you are curious, I choose to frequently use weight loss examples because I see it as a topic that is universally understood, familiar and accessible. Likely, either you or someone you know, struggles with weight loss, body image and/or fitness issues. As such, this may better help you apply the concepts in this book.

Reason #3 - Tips, Tricks and Hacks

Our love affair with *tips, tricks* and *hacks* (shortcuts), is another phenomenon that powerfully contributes to our struggles with habits and behaviors that oppose our resolution efforts.

Nearly every day I receive requests to provide *tips, tricks* and *hacks (shortcuts)* for fitness, weight loss, nutrition, fear, stress, motivation, mindfulness, procrastination and productivity. Three months ago I received one asking for tips on how to be happy in 10 minutes or less. Really!? As if happiness were a light switch to be turned on and off at will, or by pressing a few buttons. Rather, it is the indirect by-product of specific thoughts, words and actions expressed over time that contribute to the development of general happiness and achieving our goals.

I recently received a request for *tips* and *tricks* on how to have *The Talk* with your kids. If you have not had the foresight, and taken the effort to develop general bridges of communication with your children from day one, it will not be there for you to cross when you want to drive *The Talk* vehicle across.

What happens when our addiction to shortcuts, couples with the wants, desires and goals of our conditioned consumer mindset? Well, they produce offspring that are reflexively susceptible to *tips, tricks* and *hacks*.

Learn this one trick to lose belly fat.

Tips on how to score. (Maybe I'm talking sports, maybe not).

Organization and money saving hacks.

5 tips to improve motivation.

3 procrastination hacks.

Tips, tricks and *hacks* exist to beat stress, be happy, find love, make up, break up, stop smoking, eat less, earn more, lose weight, get ripped, reduce wrinkles... and the list goes on.

I know, YOU are never seduced by these pitches - I'm talking about *other people*. While reading the examples above, you are removed from the event and can therefore look at them objectively, with a rational mind, and convince yourself *I'd never fall for that!* Yet, from within the situation, in the heat of the moment, the rational centers of the brain soften.

Tips, tricks and hacks are the perfect vehicle to entice the conditioned mind of your Consumer Self to purchase products and services that look and sound great, but rarely have any value in addressing the goals of your Authentic Self. Once you wipe the slick layers of marketing goo off the product or service that is supposed to help you achieve your resolutions, you are simply left with a tool that requires YOU to power it to achieve anything.

Reason #4 - Principles Driven vs. Benefits Driven

Many people who struggle with their resolutions are not truly interested in the goal itself. They simply want the BENEFITS of being organized, spending less, saving more, losing weight, quitting smoking or falling in love, 6 of the top 10 resolutions in 2017.

Sure, most people want the benefits of being wealthy or fit, but are not sufficiently motivated to take the steps required to achieve those benefits. This distinction is why lifestyle movements such as paleo-diets are more successful than not, as they produce loyalty and lifestyle integration similar to religious movements.

Contrary to popular belief, the magic does not lie in the types of food they eat, but belief in the principles of a lifestyle built on respecting the health and fitness of their body. In turn, this leads to choices that support their **Guiding Principle** of living a healthy and fit lifestyle.

As such, paleo-enthusiasts are not primarily focused on the benefits driven goal of fitting into a pair of skinny jeans, receiving peer approval or increasing one's social currency. Instead, they are often driven by a health and fitness principle to improve how they function personally and professionally. Looking better is often a welcome by-product.

Principle driven goals create thoughts, words and actions necessary to support the objective. Not valuing the goal emotionally disconnects you from it - *your heart's not in it*. This brings us back full circle to the immense power of **Guiding Principles**, as they are what keeps us emotionally connected to our daily actions. **Guiding Principles** keep you anchored to a principle driven lifestyle capable of achieving your goals.

The question is, do you value the principle tied to the goal or simply value the benefits the marketplace and society value at that moment? **Check Your Mind!**

Chapter 5

Applications

In this chapter I will show you how to apply the advice in this book to the top 3 resolutions of 2017, using the same **Guiding Principle** for each one. In this way, I will demonstrate how these seemingly separate areas of our lives are really all connected at the level of what drives us to succeed - the heart. Recognizing this connection should empower you with a perspective that greatly simplifies achieving any personally meaningful goal.

Top 3 Resolutions of 2017*

1. Being a Better Person
2. Lose Weight / Exercise More (tied)
3. Spend Less / Save More

To begin, I will start off with a bit of rant about the new #1 resolution for 2017, *being a better person*. Mostly, the more specific the goal, the greater the likelihood of success.

*Marist College Institute for Public Opinion.

For example, the goals of *improving one's health* and *eating better* (also included in the top 10 resolutions for 2017) are much less specific and therefore not as useful as stating, *I resolve to quit smoking* and *eating fast food*, in order to achieve the same objectives of improved health and eating better.

From my perspective, the trend towards non-specific resolutions reflects our society's *everyone's a winner mentality*. This approach reframes our expectations by setting the bar so low, all you have to do is accidently trip over it to succeed. How? My general resolution of *being a better person* takes the pressure, personal responsibility and commitment off me, along with the stress to be consistent, develop new habits and skill sets, and then weave these into my lifestyle.

Instead, during the 365 days worth of opportunities I have to engage in and express my 2017 resolution, I can claim success by committing just one single act that I feel comes under the broad heading of *being a better person*. So, for the first 364 days of 2017 I can tell my employees their performance is crap. But, on the 365th day of 2017, I tell them their performance is not as bad as it usually is. Am I good, because you know, that was better? Do I get to walk away trying to fool myself or others into believing I fulfilled my resolution?

While I applaud the sentiment and principle of *being a better* person, its non-specific, general nature opens the door to a subtle, subconscious shift in one's primary objective to simply not failing at your New Year's Resolution, which is not the same as succeeding.

By using imprecise, vague language, we omit a clear cut expectation or standard. As a result, we are free to produce sub-par performance because there has been no established par or criteria to compare it to and hold ourselves accountable to. One can commit a single act of *being a better person* without actually becoming a better person overall, or when it really counts. Rather than achieving a goal that reflects a long term behavioral change that positively enhances your life, you merely meet the absolute minimum requirements of your resolution, which is made easy due to its general, non-committal nature.

Remember, in order to stick to our resolutions the heart and mind must conspire to create the causes for us to *feel like* staying to course to achieve our goals. Yet, general goals often have the feeling component removed, which is why we gravitate towards them - they are safe. A non-specific resolution is similar to a gun without bullets. Useless if your goal is to shoot something.

Our desire to protect ourselves from having to feel uncomfortable gave rise to the soft, imprecise language of political correctness. And from my perspective, general goals are one of the many distorted offspring of trying to be politically correct. Rather than communicate something to you that is specific, direct and precisely hits its mark, I try and express the same message with one-off terms that miss the mark. In this way, you do not have to feel the weight of my words and we both walk away with a semi-productive, half-hearted exchange. Due to the imprecise and ineffective language used, we will need to repeat this process many times using different, yet just as inefficient language.

Perhaps you are still struggling with my perspective on this, or maybe I have not articulated it well enough, so I will bottom line it. It's the difference between committing to doing something well or simply *not sucking* at it. All *not sucking* requires is the bare minimum amount of effort, time, consideration and attention.

Consider the term I just used - *sucking*. For many, this is felt as a more vulgar term than *doing poorly* or *not doing as well*. I used this term specifically to reinforce the power specific language has in how it makes you feel. Remember *emotion creates motion*. Rant complete.

Being a Better Person - Step One

Construct a **Guiding Principle**, a values driven statement that reflects an emotional connection to your goal. Interestingly, even this general goal can be sharpened through my process. In each of our three examples I will assign the following **Guiding Principle**, *Respect and Love for Myself and Family*.

Aside from yourself, who do you care about that would benefit from you *being a better person*? Keep in mind, alignment between what you think and feel is the single most important factor in succeeding in personally meaningful goals. You need to honestly and authentically care about the people involved. Be honest, as there is no right or wrong in this context, simply what is right or wrong for you. If what you feel or don't feel is an expression of your Authentic Self, then it has to be right for you, in this moment.

Consider that a goal of *being a better person* could have immense value to your personal or business life. If so, this becomes integrated into the **Guiding Principle** of who and what you respect and love.

To be clear, feel free to create any **Guiding Principle** you can imagine, I am merely demonstrating that the true power of a **Guiding Principle** comes from its alignment in your heart and mind.

Now think about how *being a better person* will improve the way you feel, decrease stress and create greater ease of movement in your daily activities. Next, reflect on how these personal changes within you will add value and increase the level of happiness in the lives of the people you have connected to your **Guiding Principle**.

In daily practice, consistently place your attention on the intention of *Respect and Love for Self and Family* to succeed in your goal of *being a better person.*

The circle is now complete. You have created a self-reinforcing principle that will attract thoughts, words and actions to support your *being a better person* resolution.

Being a Better Person - Step Two

Compose Yourself. You will need 3 sheets of blank paper for this exercise. On the first 2 blank sheets of paper, follow the general instructions for **Composing Yourself** previously outlined numerous times in this book.

With the 3rd sheet of paper, write your resolution, *being a better person.* Under your resolution write your **Guiding Principle** - *respect and love for myself and family.* Fill up the page alternating your resolution and **Guiding Principle.**

As you do this, hold the image in your mind of the people whose lives will be improved (including you) and how that will feel *being a better person.* Also consider how your daily victories will feel as a result of having taken actionable steps to support your goal.

So, your **Guiding Principle** aligns your goal with your heart - *emotion creates motion.* **Composing Yourself** serves three purposes. First, the "subconscious mind dump" helps remove reflexive behaviors in your subconscious that oppose you *being a better person.*

Second, it enables deposits to your subconscious that support the foundational habits of *being a better person*. Third, it provides reinforcement of daily thoughts, words and actions to support how *being a better person* improves communication in all areas of your life.

Let's look at another potent way to **Compose Yourself**. Write on a blank sheet of paper one action step to move you one step closer to *being a better person*. You will either perform this action immediately or write down what time you will perform it that day. Now re-write your action step over and over, as fast as you can, until you reach the bottom of the page. If performing immediately, get up and do it - NOW!

This is a powerful method that results in the subconscious prioritizing actions to support your resolution and **Guiding Principle**. Done first thing in the morning ensures your first thoughts, words and actions support your goals, before you focus on the rest of your day, which are typically actions that oppose your efforts.

Having said that, you can also perform this exercise anytime you feel conflicted between your goal and a habit or response that does not support your goal. The best way to discover these opposing forces is to **Check Your Mind**, which we will address next.

Being a Better Person - Step Three

The last component of your resolution success model is to **Check Your Mind** - often. This action will keep you from getting lost, as you travel towards *being a better person*. As with any journey where you consistently check directions to ensure you are getting closer to your destination, **Checking Your Mind** should be the most often used tool throughout the day.

- When constructing your **Guiding Principle, Check Your Mind** to discover what and who you honestly think and feel is important.

- **Check Your Mind** to separate your Authentic Self from your Consumer Self.

- In any given moment, do my thoughts, words and actions support or oppose my ability to *be a better person* and the values of my **Guiding Principle**? **Check Your Mind!**

- **Check Your Mind** to discover how you feel when expressing yourself in ways that that do not support *being a better person*.

Each time you create a thought, word or action that supports *being a better person*, **Check Your Mind** to acknowledge how you feel. This is your opportunity to channel your inner Bruce Lee... *absorb what is useful and discard what is useless.* This process reinforces those feelings, decreasing your conditioned resistance points, making it easier to continue this process the next opportunity you have to practice *being a better person.*

Your Resolution Success Model

Once again, the imagery you should have in your mind is a self-sustaining circle of success, driven and nourished by **Guiding Principles, Composing Yourself** and **Checking Your Mind**.

Lose Weight / Exercise More - Step One

Although for 2017 *losing weight* has lost its perennial pole position at the top of the resolutions list, it still sits firmly in the #2 position. Just as with *being a better person,* we will be using the Guiding Principle of *respect and love for myself and family.*

Aside from yourself, who do you care about that would benefit from your losing weight? It is important to distinguish between those who you don't care about, yet would benefit, from those you do care about and would also benefit. Simply including your spouse, children, significant other or siblings because they are family, and therefore believe you should include them in the circle of people you care about, but do not in context of your goal, will likely result in resolution failure.

Alignment between what you think and feel is the single most important factor in succeeding in personally meaningful goals. You need to honestly and authentically care about the person in context of your resolution, not say you care because you are supposed to or because of their title. Be honest, as there is no right or wrong in this context, simply what is right or wrong for you.

If what you feel or don't feel is an expression of your Authentic Self, then it has to be right for you, in this moment.

What is built into this declaration is an emotional anchor point rooted in how you feel about and value yourself, and those you love. For some of you, *family* extends beyond blood or marital relationships to include close friends. Remember, *emotion creates motion*, so the most important factor is how you *feel* about them, not their title.

Now consider how losing weight will improve how you feel and enhance how you look, while increasing energy, decreasing stress and creating more ease of movement in your daily activities.

Next, reflect on how these personal changes within you will add value and increase the level of happiness in the lives of the people you have connected to your **Guiding Principle**. For example, less stress means more patience for your children and an opportunity for them to model your behavior.

The circle is now complete. You have created a self-reinforcing principle that will attract thoughts, words and actions to support your weight loss resolution efforts.

Lose Weight / Exercise More - Step Two

Compose Yourself. Ideally make this the first thing you do each day, before interfacing with technology or other people. You will need 3 sheets of blank paper for this exercise. On the first 2 blank sheets of paper, begin writing as fast as you can whatever is in your head. DO NOT judge, worry about grammar, punctuation, legibility or try to make it about anything specific. This is a free flow, subconscious mind dump, from your head to paper. Curse, be profane, prolific, happy, angry, sad or silly. Let whatever is in you flow uninterrupted from pen to paper. What you write does not need to make sense, and might look or feel like inane ramblings - it's all good!

With the 3rd sheet of paper, write your resolution, *Lose Weight*. Under your resolution write your **Guiding Principle**. Fill up the page alternating your resolution and **Guiding Principle**. As you do this, hold the image in your mind of the people whose lives will be improved (including you) and how your weight loss success will feel. Your **Guiding Principle** aligns your goal with your heart - *emotion creates motion.*

Composing Yourself serves three purposes. First, the "subconscious mind dump" helps remove reflexive behaviors in your subconscious that oppose your weight loss efforts. Second, it enables deposits to your subconscious that support the foundational habits of weight loss. Third, it provides reinforcement of daily thoughts, words and actions to support your resolution.

Let's look at another potent way to **Compose Yourself**. Write on a blank sheet of paper one action step that moves you one step closer to your weight loss goal. You will either perform this action immediately, or write down what time you will perform it that day. Now re-write your action step over and over, as fast as you can, until you reach the bottom of the page. If performing immediately, get up and do it - NOW! Example actions steps can include signing up for an exercise class or program, getting up and jogging a quarter mile, or fixing a balanced, nutrient dense meal following the simple model in my nutrition book **The 3/4 Rule** (@Amazon).

This is a powerful method that results in the subconscious prioritizing actions to support your resolution and **Guiding Principle**. Done first thing in the morning ensures your first thoughts, words and actions support your goals, before you focus on the rest of your day, which often include actions that oppose your efforts.

Having said that, you can also perform this exercise anytime you feel conflicted between your goal and a habit or response that does not support your goal. You discover these opposing forces when you **Check Your Mind**.

Lose Weight - Step Three

The last component of your resolution success model is to **Check Your Mind** - often. This action will keep you from getting lost as you travel towards your weight loss destination. As with any journey where you consistently check directions to ensure you are on track to reach your destination, **Checking Your Mind** should be the most often used tool throughout the day.

- When constructing your **Guiding Principle**, **Check Your Mind** to discover what and who you honestly think and feel is important.

- **Check Your Mind** to separate your Authentic Self from your Consumer Self. Don't buy the infomercial exercise program or tool unless it is integrated into your Guiding Principle and resolution.

For example, I resolve to use the Super Duper Fat Melting Machine product every day for the next 90 days. When I struggle, I will put my attention on my GP of *respect and love for myself and family.*

- In any given moment, do my thoughts, words and actions support or oppose me losing weight and the values of my **Guiding Principle?** **Check Your Mind!**

- **Check Your Mind** to discover how you feel when you do not want to exercise or eat food that does not support your ends. There are times when you will honestly feel fine about it and should. Although you can attempt to justify actions that oppose your goals, if you do not feel good about it, your heart and mind will be out of alignment, which will derail your efforts and undermine your success.

Your Resolution Success Model

The imagery you should have in your mind is a self-sustaining circle of success, driven and nourished by **Guiding Principles, Composing Yourself** and **Checking Your Mind.**

Spend Less / Save More - Step One

We will again use the same **Guiding Principle** used for being a better person and weight loss - *respect and love for myself and family.*

Aside from yourself, who do you care about that would benefit from you spending less and saving more? Keep in mind, alignment between what you think and feel is the single most important factor. You need to honestly and authentically care about the people involved. If what you feel or do not feel is an expression of your Authentic Self, then it has to be right for you, in this moment.

Although the value of *spending less and saving more* seems obvious, take time to deeply consider all the ways this could improve your personal or business goals of helping not just yourself, but others.

Now consider how *spending less and saving more* will improve how you feel, decrease stress and give you a greater sense of control, freedom and choice in your life. Next, reflect on how these personal changes within you will add value and increase the level of happiness in the lives of the people you have connected to your **Guiding Principle**.

The circle is now complete. You have created a self-reinforcing principle that will attract thoughts, words and actions to support your *spend less and save more* resolution. While not at specific as it could be, note that *spend less / save more* is less general than simply saying *improve my finances* or *make more money.*

Caution! Resolutions primarily driven by benefits mostly fail because they emotionally disconnect the person from taking the daily action steps required to succeed. I think everyone desires the benefits of *spending less and saving more,* but do you honestly *feel like* taking the steps necessary to acquire those benefits? If you are being honest, many of you will answer no, you just want the benefits.

For those of you who feel this way, it is vital that you follow the three steps I am guiding you through. You must create a Guiding Principle that you feel like putting your attention on more than simply the benefits.

The exception are those of you who truly feel a deep emotional connection to just the benefits. If you fit this profile, then your attachment to the benefits will be in alignment with your authentic self.

Spend Less / Save More - Step Two

Compose Yourself. You will need 3 sheets of blank paper for this exercise. On the first 2 blank sheets of paper, follow the general instructions for **Composing Yourself** previously stated.

With the 3rd sheet of paper, write your resolution, *spend less / save more*. Under your resolution write your **Guiding Principle** - *respect and love for myself and family*. Fill up the page alternating your resolution and **Guiding Principle**.

As you do this, hold the image in your mind of the people whose lives will be improved (including you) and how that will feel as your financial situation improves. Also consider how your daily victories will feel as a result of having taken actionable steps to support your goal. Whether you accumulate money at home in a jar, envelope or safe, or at a financial institution, monetary goals provide the added advantage of you being able to see the tiny, daily changes that usually go unnoticed with goals such as weight loss.

Composing Yourself serves three purposes. First, the "subconscious mind dump" helps remove reflexive behaviors in your subconscious that oppose you *spending less / saving more*. Second, it enables deposits to your subconscious that support the foundational habits of *spending less / saving more*. Third, it provides reinforcement of daily thoughts, words and actions to support how *spending less / saving more* improves your general perspective on life.

Let's look at another potent way to **Compose Yourself**. Write on a blank sheet of paper one action step to move you one step closer to *spending less / saving more*. Perhaps you bring your lunch to work a few times a week, not only saving money, but also addressing any health or fitness goals you might have. You will either plan or prepare your lunch immediately, or write down what time you will do it later that day. Now re-write your action step over and over, as fast as you can, until you reach the bottom of the page. If performing immediately, get up and do it - NOW!

Although your ability to *spend less / save more* will be challenged on a daily basis, each challenge provides another opportunity to succeed and feel good about that success.

Spend some time thinking about your typical day and make a list of all your financial leaks. Bear in mind that while many daily expenditures might be small, the cumulative effect can be significant. Fortunately, this dynamic works both ways as the cumulative effect of small daily savings can also be significant.

Spend Less / Save More - Step Three

The last component of your resolution success model is to **Check Your Mind** - often. This action will help you stay on track *spending less / saving more.* **Checking Your Mind** should be your most frequently used tool to keep you connected to your **Guiding Principle** and help guide your thoughts, words and actions in support of your resolution.

- When constructing your **Guiding Principle, Check Your Mind** to discover what and who you honestly think and feel is important.

- **Check Your Mind** to separate your Authentic Self from your Consumer Self. Buying in quantity to leverage a discount is good. Justifying spending more than necessary because there is a sale is often bad.

- In any given moment, do my thoughts, words and actions support or oppose my ability to *spend less / save more*, as well as the values of my **Guiding Principle?** Check Your Mind!

- **Check Your Mind** to discover how you feel when expressing yourself in ways that that do not support *spending less / saving more*. Are your head and heart in alignment with one another.

Your Resolution Success Model

As is true with the previous resolutions discussed, *spending less / saving more* should be associated with an image in your mind of a self-sustaining circle of small daily successes, driven and nourished by **Guiding Principles, Composing Yourself** and **Checking Your Mind.**

Well my friends, it is time to literally close the book on Resolution Solution 2017 and begin taking action!

Remember, your resolution might start in your mind, but can only be fulfilled when it mixes with your heart. It is the integration of the heart and mind that enables us to *feel like* taking the action steps necessary to succeed in any lifestyle goal.

I Wish You All an Empowering Year!

About the Author

Chris Weiler is a performance expert to athletes, Fortune 500's and YOU! His background in philosophy, physics, and personal fitness/strength training, inadvertently helped provide the foundation for his unique perspectives and processes in developing habits and behaviors to maximize personal performance in all areas life.

A native of Chicago, Chris enjoys his family, kayaking, rock climbing, 4 wheeling off-road, Buddhism, burning the midnight oil, problem solving and pie. His literary heroic thinkers are Isaac Asimov, Steven Covey, Aldous Huxley, William James, Steven Levitt, George Orwell, Ayn Rand, and Dr. Seuss.